On our library shelves
with thanks to the
**Windsor Park
Parents' Association**

ituko

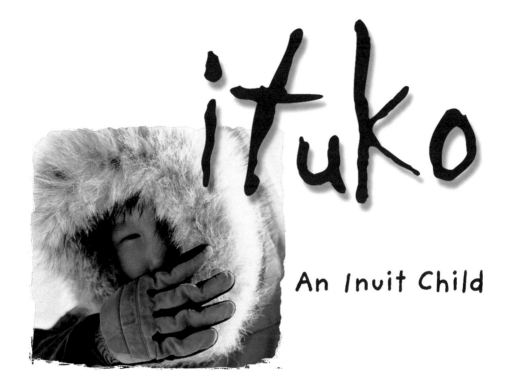

An Inuit Child

BLACKBIRCH PRESS

An imprint of Thomson Gale, a part of The Thomson Corporation

THOMSON
★ ™
GALE

Detroit • New York • San Francisco • San Diego • New Haven, Conn. • Waterville, Maine • London • Munich

For more information, contact
Blackbirch Press
27500 Drake Rd.
Farmington Hills, MI 48331-3535
Or you can visit our Internet site at http://www.gale.com

Photo Credits: Hoa-Qui/Boschung, cover, 1; Fovea-Sequoia/Barbagallo, 6, 8, 16 (left); /Rosing, 10; /Kachler, 16 (right); Ana/Johnson, 14 (left), 15 (upper right); /Weisman, 22 (bottom); Gamma/Vernay, 7, 17 (bottom), 19 (top), 20; /Todd, 13; /Halley, 14 (inset); /Lavrakas Liaison, 18; /Hallyman Liaison, 22 (top); Explorer/Chevallier, 9 (inset); Hery, 17 (top); /Gohier, 19 (bottom); /Suinot, 11 (right); /Rowell, 11 (left), 15 (left), 21 (bottom); /Boutin, 12 (inset); Holton, 12 (left); /Gayrard, 21 (top); Table of Contents collage: EXPLORER/Boutin (upper left); François Goalec (upper middle and right); Muriel Nicolotti (bottom left); CIRIC/Michel Gauvry (bottom middle); CIRIC/Pascal Deloche (bottom right)

LIBRARY OF CONGRESS CATALOGING-IN-PUBLICATION DATA

Ituko : an Inuit child.
    p. cm. — (Children of the world)
  ISBN 1-4103-0282-2 (hard cover : alk. paper)
  1. Inuit children—Social life and customs. 2. Inuit—Social life and customs. 3. Arctic regions—Social life and customs. I. Blackbirch Press. II. Series: Children of the world (Blackbirch Press)

Printed in the United States of America
10 9 8 7 6 5 4 3 2

Contents

The Arctic

ARCTIC   OCEAN

The Arctic Circle

SWEDEN

NORWAY

FINLAND

ESTONIA

RUSSIA

DENMARK

LATVIA

LITHUANIA

BELARUS

U.K. NETH.

BELGIUM GERMANY POLAND

LUX.

AUSTRIA CZECH SLOVAKIA UKRAINE

KAZAKHSTAN

MONGOLIA

SWITZ. SLOVENIA HUNGARY MOLDOVA

FRANCE

ITALY CROATIA ROMANIA

BOSNIA SERBIA BULGARIA

GEORGIA

UZBEKISTAN

NORTH KOREA

SPAIN

MONTENEGRO MACEDONIA

ARMENIA AZERBAIJAN

KYRGYZSTAN

SOUTH KOREA

ALBANIA GREECE

TURKMENISTAN TAJIKISTAN

PACIFIC

TURKEY

CYPRUS LEBANON SYRIA

JAPAN

TUNISIA

ISRAEL

IRAQ IRAN

AFGHANISTAN

CHINA

MOROCCO

JORDAN

KUWAIT

ALGERIA

LIBYA EGYPT

SAUDI ARABIA

QATAR

U.A.E.

PAKISTAN

NEPAL

BHUTAN

TAIWAN

OMAN

INDIA

MYANMAR LAOS

TANIA

MALI NIGER CHAD

SUDAN

ERITREA YEMEN

BANGLADESH

THAILAND

VIETNAM

BURKINA

DJIBOUTI

CAMBODIA

BENIN NIGERIA

PHILIPPINES

IVORY

TOGO

SOMALIA

COAST GHANA CAMEROON

CENTRAL AFRICAN

ETHIOPIA

EQUATORIAL GUINEA REPUBLIC

SRI LANKA

AO TOME & PRINCIPE

UGANDA

BRUNEI

CONGO

KENYA

MALAYSIA

GABON ZAIRE

RWANDA

SINGAPORE

ZAMBIA

BURUNDI

TANZANIA

INDIAN

INDONESIA

PAPUA

NEW GUINEA

ANTIC

ANGOLA ZAMBIA

NAMIBIA

MALAWI

FIJI

ZIMBABWE

BOTSWANA

MOZAMBIQUE

MADAGASCAR

NEW CALEDONIA

SWAZILAND

AUSTRALIA

SOUTH

LESOTHO

AFRICA

OCEAN   OCEAN

NEW ZEALAND

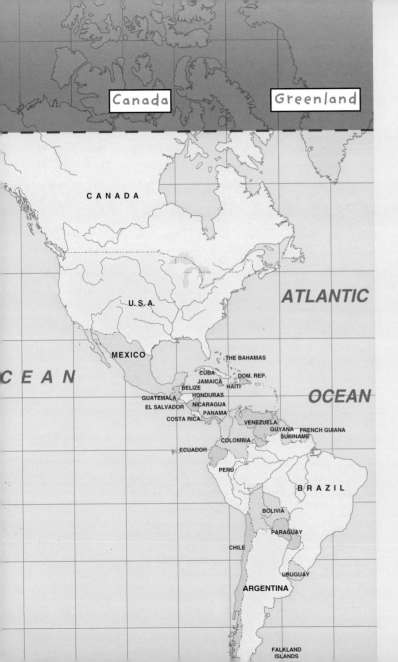

Facts About the Arctic

The territories of the Arctic surround the North Pole and cover 4,633,312 square miles (12 million square kilometers).

The Inuit:	An Asiatic people who spread into the Arctic over thousands of years.

Areas where the Inuit live:

Greenland (Denmark): 46,000
Alaska (United States): 35,000
Labrador, Nunavik (Canada): 30,000
Siberia (Russia): 1,500

Industry:	hunting and fishing
Languages:	Inupik, Inuktitut, Yupik.
Religion:	shamanism

The Arctic of the Inuit

The Arctic, the northern land where the Inuit live, is
a desert of snow and ice.

For thousands of years, the Inuit have lived in Greenland, in northern Canada, in Alaska, and in eastern Siberia.

Even the oceans are filled with ice.

The Inuit

The Inuit live in deserts of ice and snow in the Arctic. This is also the land of polar bears, seals, and caribou. They used to be called Eskimos, but they do not like to be called this anymore. In Inuktitut, an Inuit language, *eskimo* means "an eater of raw meat."

The Arctic appears bleak and lifeless but it is the home of polar bears, seals, and caribou.

Left: A blizzard.

Below: Living in such a harsh land requires the right clothing and tools.

9

The Polar Night an

In winter, the temperature can drop to 94 degrees below zero fahrenheit (70 degrees below zero Celsius). Even the ocean freezes. Piles of ice make up the icepack. In winter, the sun does not shine in the Arctic.

In Thule, Greenland, where Ituko lives, the polar night lasts from the end of October until the end of February. But the sky is lit by beautiful white, green, and red lights. These lights are called the aurora borealis, or northern lights.

In winter, icy winds blow from the north. Blizzards bring lots of snow.

In summer, the temperature warms up a little. The top surface of the earth thaws.

The aurora borealis, or northern lights, are beautiful.

the Midnight Sun

In the northernmost regions, the sun does not set from May until the end of August. At midnight, it is almost as light as the middle of the day. This is called the midnight sun.

Above: The polar night.

Right: The midnight sun.

Ituko's Village

Ituko.

I tuko is a young Inuit boy of eight. He lives with his family near Thule, Greenland. He lives with his dad, Ogni, and his mom, Noonah.

Noonah, Ituko's mom.

More than 100 people live in the village.

The wooden houses are only one story high. They have electricity, but no running water. Twice a week, a tank truck delivers water to each house.

Even if it is very cold outside, the houses are well heated thanks to oil stoves in every room.

13

Ituko's School and Friends

At school, Ituko learns English. However, his classes are also taught in Inuktitut.

Anorak, *igloo*, and *kayak* are Intuktitut words. The school uses a computer programmed in Inuktitut.

When the children leave school or home, they put on snowsuits, boots, and parkas.

In the winter, to be extra warm, they snuggle into furry caribou skin jackets.

Top: Nestled against her mother's back, a small Inuit child keeps warm in a fur-lined hood.

Bottom: When school lets out, it is playtime for the children.

Ituko likes to stay home and read, draw, or watch television. He also enjoys playing with his friends or going to the library or the skating rink.

Ituko also likes to bicycle, swing, and even go swimming with his friends when the sun is warm. The temperature of the sea is still quite cold, however.

On the Tundra

*E*ach weekend, particularly in summer, almost everyone leaves the village. They wander about and camp in cloth tents.

When Ituko is along, he likes to lie down on caribou skins and listen to Noonah.

The igloo is made up of blocks of hard snow.

While she makes hot tea, she tells him about her childhood. At that time, her family, like most Inuit of the region, did not yet live in the village.

Instead, the Inuit moved around all year. In summer, they camped in a sealskin tent. They lived in an igloo during the winter. The igloo took her father only an hour to build.

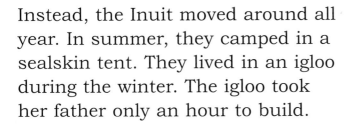

Today the Inuit still go hunting and fishing. Some ride in snowmobiles, others travel by dogsled.

Snowmobiles are replacing traditional dogsleds more and more.

Food

Butchering a whale into large pieces.

Neither vegetables nor grains can grow in the Arctic. It is just too cold. So Noonah boils meat every day, usually seal or caribou. Ituko sometimes eats fish and seabird eggs.

The store carries canned fruits and vegetables. They are brought in by plane. Noonah does not buy them. She prefers to eat the "food of the earth," food that must be caught by hunting and fishing.

Fishing

To fish, the Inuit bore holes into the icepack, which can be as much as 10 feet (3 meters) thick.

Hunting

The Inuit use harpoons to hunt whales, seals, and walrus. If they used modern guns, the Inuit would be able to kill many animals. They choose not to, though. They have passed strict hunting laws to ensure that there will be enough wild animals left for their children and grandchildren.

In the midst of a storm, Ogni ties up a seal he has just killed. Once it is secure, he drags it back to the village.

Hunting polar bears, whales, and walrus is sometimes dangerous.

Each year a few Inuit hunters disappear in the sea when they try to bring an animal that they have killed out on the ice. Some are carried away on the ice pack, while others drown.

When an animal is killed, no part is wasted. The Inuit use all the parts. They eat the meat and the fat and make clothes and bags with the skins. The bones are used to make tools, weapons, or toys.

Above: A polar bear.

Left: Women sew the animal skins.

The Future

Over the past few dozen years, the way of life of the Inuit has changed completely. These nomads once lived in igloos. Now they live in comfortable heated homes.

Left: An Inuit woman in traditional dress.

Heated homes in villages are replacing tents and igloos as Inuit life changes.

They use computers, telephones, and watch television. However, more than half the Inuit depend on money from the government.

The biggest danger facing young Inuit is alcoholism.

23

Other Books in the Series

Arafat: A Child of Tunisia

Asha: A Child of the Himalayas

Avinesh: A Child of the Ganges

Ballel: A Child of Senegal

Basha: A Hmong Child

Frederico: A Child of Brazil

Kradji: A Child of Cambodia

Kuntai: A Masai Child

Leila: A Tuareg Child

Madhi: A Child of Egypt

Thanassis: A Child of Greece

Tomasino: A Child of Peru